MERCI LANE PRESS

PULSE

Of All Things Living

Pulse of All Things Living
Copyright © 2018 Rhonda Rieck-Rush

ISBN 978-0-9967884-9-6
Published by Merci Lane Press

CONTENTS

LANTERN

Night owls' eyes like stars
pastures like flowing rivers
full moon my lantern

(won 6th place in Lincoln Underground's haiku contest,
summer 2016)

ARRIVAL OF AUTUMN

Autumn arrived tapping
at the windows,
pitter-pattering atop my roof,
drenching changing trees,
gushing from rain gutters,
forcing small streams
across the lawn.
Fall has announced
its presence and said to summer,
"we shall meet same time next year".

NATURE'S APPLAUSE

Leaves applauding in the
shimmering sunlight
celebrating nature's bounty
the harvest now done
fields lie barren but a grain
or kernel or husk
dust bowls rise and swirl
down old country roads

MOONSTRUCK

Behold her round and glowing beauty
like a large golden wafer in the sky;
how she dips her brilliance into dark
rivers, keeping them warm and
alive, flowing like blood through the
veins of earth. The depths mirror
moons' glistening light like a thousand
tiny prisms capturing her stark
reflection as her particles disperse over
waters' surface. She fills in the waves
and ripples with her gleaming presence,
her colors bleed into nights' canvas,
dazzling and enticing her audience to
recognize her changing mood and how
she loves this time of year.
(first published in spring 2016 issue of Plainsongs)

2

PARTLY CLOUDY

Wispy waves of white
swirling in ocean blue sky
brush strokes from heaven

CANVAS

Skin is the canvas
of our experiences
living tapestry

CICADA TREES

Instrumental wings
a chorus of cicada
trees singing their song

TANGERINE SUNSET

Tangerine Sunset
spills her incandescent light
into turquoise streams

OCEAN DEEP

An ocean of words
trapped in a single teardrop
I refuse to cry

CONFIRMATION OF SPRING

Young fawns' spindly legs
her soft, pearly white freckles
spring's confirmation

RURAL PASSION

Ride down old dirt roads
witness passionate farmers
cultivate their land

the sprinkling of seeds
life, the product of their hands
nurturing our earth

GREEN(ery)

Green is GO,
    and growth,
        and renewal. It's fresh like
blades of grass bulldozing earth,
    buds of leaves unfolding.
Green is a crisp spring salad,
    stem of a strawberry,
        peppers dangling like ornaments,
            watermelon rinds.
Green is life's envelope opening, you and I fixated
        on every scent and scene and
                poem we might create.

NATURE'S BREATH

If I could sit beside a brook
      among lush green shade trees
and the wild tall grass,
I'd listen to waters rush over rock,
      hear bubbles rise from
mouths of tadpole
frogs leap in shallow stream
plop, plop
      their croaking throats
singing in mid morning sun,
celebrating renewal of life...
cattails bowing to the wind,
leaves rustling in spring's breeze,
wispy waves of cottony skies
casting shadows across the plains
dragonflies, like pendulums swaying
      above rippling waters,
songbirds calling, wings reaching
      for heavens hand to guide them
yellow jackets' happy buzz...
And, if I put my ear to the ground,
    I hear night crawler digging tunnels
and blades of grass bulldozing earth,
      their roots anchoring firm in
rick, deep, black soil
nature in sync with
all creatures, everything
      alive and breathing,
      me, taking it all in.

MINI GALAXY

Blink of lightning bugs
microscopic satellites
caught in mason jars

DEPARTURE OF SUMMER

Summer now in my rear view,
I reminisce of hot summer days,
days that rose me from by bed early
       and kept me out late,
days when the hot pavement
made me walk more briskly,
days that painted
    my pale skin bright red, and days
the hungry heat consumed my
    popsicle before I got the chance.
The sun now calling it a day
much sooner and sleeping in
    later each morning; for this change
of season is necessary for rebirth.

LOST MATE

Like a lonely songbird
in a foreign land, her mate
she cannot find.
Her notes fall on distant canvas
without a reply;
she is isolated from love
and bears the emptiness
with her instrument as
her sole navigator.

INNOCENCE

My inner child does not fear
the depths of this journey, but
welcomes its mystery,
ponders its beauty, and
explores its boundaries...
oh, if only I could return to
thy innocence.

MY OBSERVATION COMING HOME FROM THE LIBRARY

Dove mates peck at the cobblestone streets
in the middle of my path home.

A medium-haired tabby strolls from the curb
and across the road just ahead.

Young squirrels, unaware the danger, leap
in front of traffic playing a game of tag.

Cars and trucks zoom by without a care,
taking folks to and from their destinations, often
impatient; unlike the animals, who only seem
intruding, who aren't hurried by anything
but the blazing of car horns.

Oh, if only people could be so content.

FORECAST

Weatherman forecasts
patchy with a chance of rain
what a lovely quilt

SENSUOUS NATURE

Let me gaze at the
oceans in your eyes,
see the bounty of your
splendid landscape,
trace the curves of
your mountains with
my fingertips,
hike your canyons and
your valleys,
smell the fragrance of
your petals, the scent of
your sweet layers.
Let me listen to
the whispers of your
imagination,
hear the thump of
your emotion,
taste the dew of
nature rising
and waterfalls spilling
over your cliffs.

WEB

Lost in solemn thought
entangled in daydream's web
freedom imagined

DRAGONFLIES

Metallic bodies
dragonflies like pendulums
swaying in warm breeze

NEBRASKA RANGE

I yearn for open country

where the sky goes clear to your feet
and landscape is not marred
by high rises and city lights
that conceal sun's rise and fall
and hide the twinkling stars

where, if you listen closely,
can hear limbs of trees
stretching towards heaven,
their expanding roots creating
miniature earthquakes beneath your feet.

I yearn for open country

where short-eared owl roosts
in old transparent barns and
cattle graze in green pastures

where garter snake slithers through
fields and competes for what
old owl hunts

where prairie grass ripples
golden waves across endless plains
in the mid-day sun

I long for this Nebraska range
                    where I feel free.

FALL OUTLOOK

I gaze upon the change
occurring outside my window
reminiscing about the many
summers I've bid farewell
but welcoming the shedding
of old skins and how they've
become translucent

PROMISING SKIES

Clouds laced in gold-trimmed edges
skies as blue as oceans
suns' rays beaming forth new hope

WINTER CABIN

Gather near fireplace
dismiss winter's frozen breath
crackling flame, hypnotizing

Twinkling embers pop
like flickers of lightning bugs
reviving warm memories

COLD SEASON'S END

Winter has unclenched
the thaw now weeks behind us
leaves and wings unfold

SPRING'S LAUNCH

Launching into spring
butterfly gardens commence
the zoo is open

SPRING'S KISS

Winter's icy breath
inhales spring's sweet aroma
from blossoms' first kiss

OLD BARN

Old transparent barn
sways slightly
with spring's shifting breeze
(1st published in Misbehaving Nebraskans, an anthology
2017)

CRESCENT MOON

Sliver of moonlight
winks at passing cumulus
like boatloads of tired tourists

TIMBER

Rooftop chatter speaks
about the absent branches
which use to be home

all that's left is stump
where once their tree contested
to being lifeless

for, though itself dead
found creatures still inhabit
its aged hollow trunk

BLOOM

Budding
velvet petals
full bloom

TINY WINGS

Hatchlings
birds ' tiny wings
unfold

SAVED BY FIRE (Joseph's Star poem)

Flame
twigs popping
smoke rising through haze
a blanket of warmth surrounds
dead leaves crackle in the fire
rescuers spot hope
signs of life
saved

PROMISE OF A CHILD

The soft whisper
of your heartbeat
caresses my imagination;
lost in pleasant daydream
of what you may become
and how you've already
changed the world.

RIPPLES=MORSE CODE

Casting off from shore
bobbers plunge in murky lake
sending secret codes

NO CATCH

Winding in my pole
bobber skips across water
as I reel in bare hook

TUG OF WAR

Tugging at my line
large bluegill slurps night crawler
yet, declines the hook

EVENING GLIDING LESSON

Young falcon floats
through eve's mandarin sky
riding her coattails

DUSK

Edge of horizon
sun's fire slowly suffocates
earth swallows last light

NIGHT COURT

Moon adjourns
black silk sky disrobes
to daybreak
(1st published in Misbehaving Nebraskans, an anthology
2017)

NIGHT SHOWER

Celestial bodies
illuminate night's dark sky
nature's bold fireworks

GARDEN PARTY

Garden ants gather
to feast on green melon rinds
after late picnic

SUMMER PARADE

Marching single file
an ant colony's kick-off
to summer's parade

ANCHOR

You are the anchor
which keeps me from drifting far
in treacherous seas

FALL TORNADO

Complexion of fall
swirls in leafy tornadoes
season's last downpour

RAIN

A spasm of rain
droplets of tiny oceans
microcosmic splash

SEARCHING FOR THE RING

I walk along a ditch
on the side of a gravel road
in a familiar countryside
kicking an occasional pebble
ducking low-hanging limbs
stepping cautiously
keeping my eyes peeled
for the shimmering stone
atop a parched earth
(it hasn't rained in weeks)
searching for the ring
I flung from my car window
the night before
when I decided it was over.

SEASON'S SWEET RETURN (a lune poem)

Bloom of wildflowers
nectar sweet
butterfly gardens

FENCES

Fence posts like matchsticks
imperfectly parallel
taming wild horses

LEAVING CITY LIFE

I am departing this lonesome city,
making my way back to where
my roots are embedded deep.
I won't miss the smog, the heavy traffic,
the fast pace, people fighting
through crowds or fighting the fatigue,
people so self-absorbed,
proud and arrogant.
I am done with the deceitful glamour
my soul longs for the simplicity
of neighbors being neighborly,
people paying attention to what's important.
I'm leaving this dreadful, polluted city
so I can again be among folks who know
what keeping promises mean.

RETIRING FARMER

Old wagon wheel propped against
a weathered farmhouse,
retired from traveling country roads.
Old barn tilting north,
beaten by many a storm,
yet withstanding all of its cruelty.
Old timer still packing his pipe
with tobacco while surveying
his fields and taking inventory.
Old letters from his children
who went off to college
and never returned.
Old sorrows bottled up and
sent downstream in a current
to eventually rest beneath the riverbed.
Old memories, he reminisces,
feeding translucent film through
the projector of his mind.
Old gravestone at the foot
of a large cottonwood
beside the riverbank.
Old crooked fingers tracing
her name, Lucille Baker,
Loving Wife and Mother.
Old bones ever weary
ready to relinquish and
be born to something new.

FAMILY FARM

The loose slats of floorboard creek and moan
as Nana rows the old wooden rocker
to and fro on the gray porch, as though
the shifting weight of her heavy bones
were agonizing reminders of all the burdens
this aged house has bore through the years.

The rotting lumber has swelled with fierce rains
and been parched by severe drought, withstood
the company of many children along with
their elders and welcomed a weary farmer after
long days in the fields when he slouches in
that old chair, lulled to sleep by evenings' breeze.

The joists are now sagging with age, her seams
have come undone while the sloping roof pulls
inward. Shutters bang against the farmhouse
when gusts of wind hammer her weakened frame
and toss tumbleweed across a scorched earth
which grieves the loss of the year's crops.

Gone now is that old farmer, his children have
paved a different road, far away from this country,
seeking validation in noisy, crowded pubs inside
populated cities, groaning about how they
have not slept in ages, how they are consumed by
the demands of work and raising their own children.

Then, one September day they return to that old
farmhouse where their parents had raised them to
always do right by folks, taught them the value of

hard work and the meaning of loving your neighbors.
And, they brought with them their own children to
help them bring that old farmhouse to life again.
And, when Nana heard their cars veering down
the graveled driveway, she hurried to meet them on
that creaky porch, the screen door slapping shut
behind her as she wipes her wrinkled hands on a
dish towel, a whiff of strawberry rhubarb pie still
clinging to her floral apron, wafting from the house.

Dust settles when the cars shift into park and one
by one, her children and grand-children slip out to
greet her. They've come with hugs and kisses and
appetites for the banquet grandma has spread out on the
dining table which Papa built by hand many years
back, when he had a knack for such things.

Nana has the youngsters set out the good china and
silverware, they gather 'round that long oak table,
grasp one another's hands and bow their heads for grace.
Then, passing platters and serving bowls, the basket of
buttermilk biscuits, they eat to their fill when
Nana announces, "it's time to sell the farm…pie anyone?"

ROBIN

Robin comes searching
the freshly mown lawn
for a feast of worms

THUNDERSTORM

Thunder rolls through skies
like multiple explosions
striking lightning flames

YARD WASTE

Grass clippings
swept away by rain
green river

BUG BITES

Tiny swallows
glide across still waters
snatching insects

SNOWFLAKES

Sparkling gems
descend from
winter's sky

WINTER FAIRIES

She presses her tiny nose
against the cold pane
her breath fogs the window
then she tilts away from
the glass and places
her index finger where
she has left her cloud and
with a swirling motion
traces a path where little
fairies can fly.

WINTER SUNRISE

A cordial invite
to rise up from my slumber
stretch and breathe deeply
scent of pine and peppermint
this crisp, wintry morn

MINI VACATION TO TAYLOR'S FALLS

In the summer of 2010 my family and I set out on a different kind of adventure, something new and exciting outside of the Twin Cities, away from the constant buzz of heavy traffic, high rises and city lights. It would be a first experience for all of us, a treasured memory that I have not forgotten to this day and will likely cherish for years to come.

The trip took us north and slightly east, zigzagging through rural Minnesota. I drove the less traveled highways as we made our way toward Taylor's Falls and the St. Croix river, which forms the border of Wisconsin and Minnesota. Our minivan was at full capacity with my husband, my three teenagers and two of their friends, me in the driver's seat with a map close by so we wouldn't get lost. The landscape was serene, the air less contaminated out here.

We followed a country road through an elegant forest of trees and into a gravel parking lot with fewer than a dozen vehicles. A tiny shack stood near the sandy beach along with silver canoes and brightly colored kayaks lined up in a row nearby, green, red, yellow, and two shades of blue. Everyone got out of the van and headed towards the water as I made my way to the little shack where I paid for three canoes. The kids were eager to begin the journey down the St. Croix River, my oldest two pairing up with their friends while my husband, youngest daughter and I shared a canoe.

My son and his friend were the first to strap on their life vests and jump ahead of the rest of our small group. My oldest daughter and her girlfriend teased one another, giggling anxiously as they tried to keep the canoe from tipping while they each climbed in. I sensed there was competition brewing between the girls and the boys.

With our life vests on, my husband and I were seated one on each end and my youngest girl in the center of our canoe. We pushed off from shore and prepared to paddle 7 miles down the river. The weather was overcast, patchy clouds occasionally blocking the sun, humid, but mild, temperatures in the low 80's.

28

A light drizzle dampened our skin just moments after our departure, but didn't derail our plans for a fun-filled family voyage and ceased as quickly as it had begun.

The boys seemed to be masters at rowing down the river swiftly while the girls tried to figure out how to use the paddles to steer the canoe in the direction they wished to go. But, we were in no hurry really, just enjoying the peace and quiet of nature surrounding us on all sides. I wanted to take our time, not feel hurried by anything.

To our left was Wisconsin, Minnesota on the right. A couple of miles into our journey we came to a small island smack in the middle of the river. One by one, we each rested our canoes on the miniature island while we stretched our legs and dipped our bare feet into the warm, shallow water, burrowing our toes in the sand. I took some snapshots of the kids and of my husband with my digital camera. My eldest daughter's friend snapped a picture of me and my 3 kids standing side by side near the river. We stood and admired the view, the rocky red cliffs along the waters' edge, lush green trees towering high on each side, cottony white clouds casting shadows on the river as they moved through blue skies, and the winding river flowing downstream towards our destination. Then, we piled back into our canoes and rowed with the current.

Pulling our ores into the canoe, we briefly allowed the river to take over while we drifted downstream. I spread my fingers apart as I immersed my hands into her wet tranquility, seizing the moment, welcoming the peace this place offered. Nature seems to have a way of calming the inner storms that rage inside of us so often, our doubts and frustrations, our inadequacies and fears. Nature touches a part of us that we fail to give heed to-our souls, life's compass, that needle which guides us and puts us back into alignment with creation and with God. Much of the time, we get caught up in our mundane routines, letting deadlines and schedules consume us, and we neglect to nourish our souls. This trip was much needed nourishment.

As we approached the final leg of our trek on the St. Croix, I lose myself in daydream-of pitching a tent around a crackling

29

campfire in this wilderness and staying for a night or two, gazing up at a galaxy of stars while sprawled out on my blanket, hands tucked underneath my head, listening to creatures stir amidst the river. I dread returning to the city. Nothing is the same there. My mood starts to shift as we inch our way to shore. Endings can be hard, especially when something so beautiful, so calming and reassuring must come to a close.

Young game and parks employees waded out at the stopping point, ready to haul in canoes and kayaks, asking how we enjoyed our journey as we climbed out and removed our life jackets. For me, it was over much too soon. Several folks had come in moments before us, waiting to board a bus which would return us to where we had parked. The kids were smiling and satisfied, as were me and my husband, happy to have shared the experience. It gave us respite from the ordinary chaos we've adapted to, living in a metropolitan area. It gave me some much needed time with my family as well as refreshment for my soul. I shall revisit the memories often and enjoy the peace they exude, where I appreciate the solitude of nature and how it puts us back in touch with ourselves.

THE NIGHTMARE

A path illuminated by moon's light
through a deceased forest
                of crippled, naked limbs.
The eerie stillness reminds me of
                death and cold bones.
The silence is interrupted
only by beating wings
                of a bat and horses' hoofs
pounding the earth. Then, I awake to
realize the noise is my heart telling me
                I'm not dead yet.

WHAT I MIGHT DO ALONE

I ponder the things I might do
if I were alone...

I'd remove the noise,
dim the lights, and
                light a candle or two

watch fireflies dance
          in the dark near my porch
while enjoying the moonlit hue

I'd open a book
            or two or three
read the bible clear through

write a novel, perhaps
              a best seller,
and write a letter to you

about how I longed to see you
           again and miss the days
when you were near

and think about
           how lonely I am
wishing you were here.

GIVE ME MY QUIET PLACE

I seek a quiet place today
where I am not enslaved to
the ticking of someone
else's clock, where its hands
do not hold me in place,
where I can let the waves
of life recede for a while and
the rifts mend on their
own time,
where I must neither accept
nor reject, rationalize or contend,
where burden don't exist and
where I feel neither defeat nor
bitterness.
I seek a quiet place to rest my
weary soul and find solace in
things undisturbed,
not marred with the scars of
all that failure and regret have
caused, where I first tasted pain
and learned you can't believe
everything you see and hear,
somewhere not contaminated
with foul talk and human error,
somewhere where innocence
isn't lost and things truly are
as they appear.
I seek a quiet place today
without shame or guilt or
hard-learned lessons, where I
can be alone, yet not lonely.

SUN TEA

Pitcher of sun tea
ripens in the summer heat
on my balcony

ice cubes clink in glass
I stir in lemon slices
a squeeze of sunshine

then pour the amber
liquid into mason jars
and sip some with you

SUMMER AT THE LAKE

Splashing in the golden ripples
of a summer sunset,
feeling the silky sands between
my toes, the light breeze
caressing my bare skin..
skipping stones across the
pewter lake and hearing her
gulp down the weight of each one.
A wisp of wings glides overhead,
announcing the arrival of dusk..
yet, moon and stars only invite
a child's gaze and ponderings
of tomorrow.

HE DISPOSED OF MY BEAUTIFUL MESS

He chopped down my purple cone flowers I'd planted in early fall, hoping for a lovely accent on the east side of my house the following summer. They had gotten rambunctious and multiplied quite nicely, though they flopped over as many have a tendency to do while their top heavy hats burst wide open. These dazzling jewels attract many winged creatures, from bees and butterflies to a wide variety of birds. But, he has little appreciation for such things, thinks of them as a nuisance. I, on the other hand, adore such beautiful messes.

OVERNIGHT AT PAWNEE

July 29, 2017-My youngest daughter and I decide to get away for the evening, an impulsive last minute decision really. I was requiring some solitude, much needed peace and quiet away from the familiar, mundane routine my husband is quite content to engage in, as with all of his weekends, when work doesn't ask for his presence. We are polar opposites in this regard—I love silence and thrive in a quiet environment, where I can concentrate on my favorite pass-times, reading and writing. He, on the other hand, always has a cup within his grasp, full of his intoxicating brew, whether it be vodka or the occasional whiskey or rum, and the music blaring from his cheap dollar store speakers or the TV channel on some drama-filled reality show with large-breasted babes like Love and Hip-Hop or Housewives of Atlanta or some such nonsense. Neither of these is my cup of tea. So, in order to avoid the noisy clamor filling my house, we decide to drive out to a local state park and pitch my 3-man tent to spend the night near the lake.

The drive alone offers us a breath of fresh air. If I could retreat to the country on weekends, I'd be much more productive in finishing at least one of my books. I wouldn't mind an office in the upper half of an old barn for that matter, given I'd have a view of the wide open landscape and some light to write by…and a cool breeze would be a welcome luxury in these summertime temps. One of those tiny houses planted in the center of a field would be perfect. I could seriously spend the rest of my life in a tiny house, hitch it to the back of my old pick-up truck (as if I have one) when I wanted a change of scenery and just mosey on down the road. That would really get the writing juices flowing. I'd truly thrive in a serene, tranquil natural environment. It would give me the opportunity to create an oasis of lovely poetry.

We arrive at our destination on the western banks of Pawnee Lake, quickly unravel the tent before we lose daylight, and stake it into place. I unfold our chairs and place them in front of the tent, facing the water. Then, I pour charcoal briquettes in the fire pit-style grill and deuce them with lighter fluid. We've brought some turkey dogs and beans, but forgot the can opener; so much for having a balanced meal. We also have jumbo Marshmallows and skewers to roast them over the hot flames, but we have a difficult time keeping the coals burning; I should've just got the name brand charcoal instead of going the cheap route.

I listen to boats roaring out on the lake, a few jet skis skittering across the water, and an occasional fish leap above the surface near the rocky shore, creating ripples. An older man is posed on a massive concrete block tossing in his fishing line. He stays 'til the sun goes down when he loses light, having only caught several small fish, maybe baby bass or bluegill, and tossed them back. I sit and write while I have the chance before darkness sets in around us. The oil lamp is smoking and its glass turns black; perhaps we weren't supposed to vent it. At least I thought to bring a small flashlight.

My daughter has already furnished our tent with blankets and sleeping gear and she was wise to spray us with insect repellent when we first arrived; the gnats and mosquitos are swarming out here. The air is still and temps are pleasant this evening. I grab the tape deck and a cassette from my bag, borrowed to me by my client who prefers the old-school way of listening to music. The headphones are taped together but they put out sound well enough. I pop the tape in and press PLAY. I can hear the heads feed the tape through and slowly the sounds of rushing water and birds chirping begin. Immediately, I imagine a rain forest and a waterfall; it's a tape with nature sounds, then musical instruments join in, a piano, perhaps a flute. Now this is music, unlike the garbage my husband listens to, the reference to lady parts and recreational drugs, the vulgar and explicit language, the "N" word over emphasized again and again, tasteless and discriminatory to my ears. I much prefer soft noise such as on this cassette tape.

We settle in to our sleeping bags and scroll through our cell phones one last time before shutting our eyes for the night. I post a picture to Facebook of me and a marshmallow. Again, I listen to nature, what is just outside this time. The cicadas are buzzing, crickets are calling, and I am about to hum along in my dreams as my eyes get heavy and slowly close. My daughter lets out a sigh and lets this peace sink in.

REASON FOR BEING ("I am" series haiku written at the time
of the total eclipse, Aug. 21, 2017)

I am seed and sun
origin of existence
Universal God

I am earth and sky
yet no less celestial
when heaven grows dim

I am golden ring
assurance of the promise
of love eternal

I am molecule
speck of light and energy
shining galaxy

I am grain of sand
sifted through ocean's fingers
borrowed to the shore

Almighty Father
I am the magnetic force
drawing you closer

I am GOD, maker
of all divine creation
source of salvation

HELLO MOON

Hello moon…
Won't you come in?
wrap me in moonbeams
clear up to my chin

I welcome your presence
your soft, liquid light
how you seep through my window
and guard over night

we can stay up and chat
or sit quietly here
enjoying this silence
while rest draws me near

would you make me a promise
should I dose off to sleep
to come back tomorrow
and keep watch over me?

your glow calms my spirit
embraces my soul
you're a blanket of comfort
where peace overflows

so, I'll blow you a kiss
as you cradle me tight
while inviting sweet dreams
and a splendid good night

GOOD DAY SUN

Good day sun…
what a pleasant surprise
to greet me so early
with dazzling skies

you creep o'er horizon
an irrefutable flame
igniting the day
and singing my name

I jump out of bed
and open the blinds
let your rays pour in
as your happiness shines

you brighten the room
with your radiant light
immerse me in gladness
renewing my sight

should the clouds emerge
and this day grow dim
would you send a reminder
that you'll shine once again

and, before you retreat
at the end of the day
I will pause to reflect
and cast worry away.

COASTING ALONG

I coast along in a gentle breeze,
pedaling against her breath,
grasping the handlebars tightly
so as not to steer off the narrow
dirt path.

Blue jays squawk and dive bomb
a nearby intruder, a squirrel
who insists on accumulating
every acorn and seed for itself,
chattering back defensively.

Briefly, I stop and lean my
bicycle against a hollowed
tree truck and suck air deep
into my lungs, listening to
the sounds of this serene and
magical landscape.

I ask myself, 'why did we
venture so far away from such
places and when did we decide
to burrow in cities clear up to
our necks and forget about
these pieces of nature?'

Sunlight seeps through the
branches and shrubs, laying
shadows on mossy ground,
ripening the blooms, and
accentuating the scenic hues.
I bow my head and thank God.

CHILD MEMORIES

I came from humble beginnings, growing up in small Nebraska
farm towns where everyone knew everyone else's business;
gramma Dot knew all the juicy gossip in Boone County. There
were 4 of us, I being the eldest child, 2 brothers and a baby sister.
Back then, life was not so complex; we created our own fun, used
our imaginations, found ways to entertain ourselves.
We didn't stay cooped up in the house all day staring at a screen
on our tablets or smartphones, wearing out the joints of our
fingers from playing downloaded video games or scrolling
through newsfeed or YouTube pages; that stuff didn't exist then.
Instead, we went outdoors.

In summer, we stole clothes pins from the clothes line out back
and fastened a playing card or two onto our bicycle spokes,
zipping up and down the streets of our tiny town, our bicycles
magically transforming into helicopters; it's no wonder we never
had a full deck of cards. Once, I even rode my bike to the next
town over, mom following close behind in the car.
Many sunny days, I'd pull the laces tight on my dingy white
roller skates and breeze down bumpy sidewalks. We learned
about the world by flipping through the pages of books or
encyclopedias, not typing in the google search bar for instant
gratification.
We collected chokecherries alongside dirt roads in ice cream pails
and took them home so ma could whip up a batch of chokecherry
jam, so yummy on a warm English muffin. We searched the night
skies from the hood of our car, watching for shooting stars or
blinking satellites; sometimes the stars would wink at us, the
night air cool and crisp, the aroma of cattle and fields clinging to
our clothes and that raggedy quilt spread out on our old Audi.
Back then, we didn't mind letting the mysteries of the universe
remain mysteries and be in awe until the world demanded us to
grow into adults and question how it all came to be and challenge
our faith, and convinced us to believe that more is better.

BUTTERFLY GARDENS

Bloom of wildflowers
nectar sweet
butterfly gardens

STRAWBERRY ICE CREAM

Red jelly ribbons
a scoop of strawberry bliss
cold, sweet ruby swirls

SMUDGED IMAGES

The tearful glass has smudged his image,
distorted the dreams I once dreamed
a lifetime ago for us.
Time has chiseled away at our early
ambitions, drowned them in a slick
puddle that weighs down our weary souls.
But the storms we've muddled through
have washed us clean of past regrets and
made us blossom...
only in opposite directions.

MY VALENTINE SURPRISE

A crystal vase of yellow roses stands
on my window ledge soaking in the
rays of sunlight, each bud in full
bloom, every petal open to receive
the kiss of light and warmth,
scattering sweet fragrance about the room.

Lovely, sunny smiles of soft yellow
petals with pink-rimmed edges,
perky and dazzling as fine jewels,
their radiant heads flexing towards
heights of the majestic azure skies
and savoring every morsel of sun.

SILVER DOLLAR PLANET

Moon, a silver coin
lies lazily across a ribbon
of black velvet sky

A stream of somber clouds
creep slowly past her shiny face
in search of absolution

CLEVER DREAMERS

A thumbnail of light in
a dark denim sky
was barely sufficient to
walk the dirt path behind
our drafty barn
the old, red barn leaning
into a field of soybeans.
Horses in their stalls
for the night—our slithering
around in the dark
might've spooked them, the
ruckus surely would've
awakened Ma and Pa...
but we were just clever
enough to avoid rousing
those four-legged creatures,
clever enough to
lie dreaming in the hay.

FIRST LOVE

We drape the quilt
my grandmother stitched
across the hood of your
old Caprice.

Our legs intertwine, you wrap me
in your strong, tender arms,
kiss my forehead gently with
your soft, reassuring lips.

You've become my armor against
all the world threatens to steal,
my shield from the wars raging
around us, the calm of a storm
which brews within..

You are my watchman, my anchor,
the one who has vowed to cease
this loneliness I have carried too long.

FLYING HOME

I hover above
 a billow of seafoam skies,
   a mound of lamb's wool,
     a blizzard of cottony fields,
       a spongy layer of meringue,
         a frothy mug of cappuccino;

Passenger of a short flight
from Denver,
a bird in these
          glorious,
                delectable
                      clouds.

STRENGTH

Strength can be measured by our ability
to withstand the storms of life.
Strength is facing defeat with a smile,
persisting after a million rejections,
moving beyond our most painful moments
and still pacing ourselves for the race.

SPRING CLEANING

I've been busy sweeping
dust bunnies into piles
clearing cobwebs from
ceiling tiles
decluttering and reorganizing
renewing and prioritizing
collecting jars of pennies
and jars of words
painting dreams
and planting verbs
now in summers' midday heat
springs' tasks still incomplete

A WALK THROUGH THE NEIGHBORHOOD

The dandelions have gone to seed.

trees, like giant green umbrellas,
stand in rows along city streets,
obviously proud of their fine apparel.

purple iris dance happily in the rain,
their mouths wide open and
their flashy tongues savoring each drop.

a hydrangea bush is erupting like a
volcano of miniature cumulus, white globes
dangling like perfect ornaments.

the peonies resemble enormous rubies,
round goblets of red wine,
layers of fragrant crimson opening…

enough beauty to write a poem.

LIVING WATER

Feel the pulse of the river
as your feet wade out
away from her shoreline,
the gentle nudge, an ever
faint tug at your ankles,

her persuasive chants
like seductive songs,
rumors enticing your soul.
you try to resist, yet you
continue to tread deeper,
stand in the center of her while
your body strains and stiffens
against her powerful current,
attempting to hold your ground.

    yet, she is relentless.

you are a fish driven downstream,
a fetus swimming inside her womb,
sloshing around in her wet belly,

until she concludes you are not hers

so the river aborts you,
spits you out
  like spoiled milk
    onto the grainy shore.

LYING AWAKE AT NIGHT

Sometimes I lie awake at night

after a projectile of light pierces the window
    maybe the headlights of an old Buick
        or a bolt of lightning

after a booming sound vibrates the glass
    perhaps the loud base of car speakers
        or the rattle of a moving freight train

Will I wake the neighbors below me
    if I stumble out of bed and walk nude across
        the creaky hardwood floors?

Will I startle the budgies in their cage,
    beaks tucked into feathers,
        one claw grasping the perch?

Will the tulips become anxious
    and begin to open
        prematurely before dawn?

If I turn the wheel, does not everything within it
begin to move?

RAIN STORM

First was the distant thunder,
the clashing of cymbals,
violent, feverish tremors,
a rumbling late-night hunger.

Then came the lightning,
sudden flashes strike
causing cracks in the black
porcelain sky, a hemorrhaging vessel.

Soon, rain spilled out of heaven,
gushing from ominous clouds,
pounding leaves like piano keys,
unleashing a musical masterpiece.

The storm, a collection of notes,
each element an instrument,
ensemble of brilliant performance,
a beautifully composed love song.

NIGHT PEARL

I held the moon in my palm,
that glossy yolk of midnight,
exquisite golden pearl

I swallowed her whole,
tilted back my head and let
her slide down like Jell-O

I tasted her sweetness, ripe
like an affectionate kiss,
a trusted and patient lover

I simply unclenched my fists,
opened my hand, and
accepted this bead of hope.

NOT FAR FROM YESTERDAY

Ma scooped a handful of clothespins from a topless milk jug and slid them inside the pocket of her floral apron, worn so thin in places that it was nearly transparent. She snatched up the fruit crate, which served as a laundry basket, from the slanted floorboards, whisked it out through the screen door and towards the clothes line in one fare swoop, the screen slapping shut rudely. Ma secured bed linens to the line as gusts of hot summer wind teased her loosely pinned auburn hair and creeped between her slender limbs giving her dress a violent twirl.

Pa packed his pipe with tobacco as his hazel eyes glanced up at her, squinting every time the wind hurled dust particles into the sultry air. He shielded the end of his pipe after striking a match and drew in a long breath; the harsh sting of tobacco burning my throat when he released it from his lungs. Pa winked at me as I turned towards him, me wrinkling my nose whenever he took a puff and blew rings of smoke from his oval shaped mouth. He studied how Ma craned her neck, how she stood on her toes reaching with her delicate hands to fasten bed sheets in rows.

I sat on the porch step combing snarls from my doll's dull blonde hair, admiring her piercing blue eyes; how I wished I had eyes that color, a shade of sky blue, but mine were green like Ma's. My skin was fair like hers too, and my hair amber as the malt liquor Pa occasionally drank after supper. Freckles trailed across the bridge of my nose, like tiny footprints in white sand; I dreamed of being on an ocean beach one day, leaving footprints that way. Ma said I had a wild imagination.

The rope of my tire swing twisted and tangled in the wind, spinning the tire until it beat against the trunk of that old oak. Windmill blades looked as if they'd fly off into the side of the chicken coop, maybe tacking one of the laying hens up by the neck; I imagined the blood spatter and Ma plucking feathers and frying the unfortunate bird in a cast iron skillet for supper.

My mind was full of little curiosities then, like a cellar full of buried treasures waiting to be unearthed or an attic with aging remnants of my ancestors packed away in cardboard boxes. But, I desired something more of the world, to go beyond the fence of our property and see the places in National Geographic magazine, those exotic lands, perhaps from where my kin had originated, so opposite of where I grew up, determined to lay my own path. And, now that I've had the chance to travel afar, when I return to this familiar piece of the world, these memories plant me into yesterday once more.

REDEMPTION IN A RAINSTORM

I have dreamed of standing
in the soft grass
nude and unrestrained
lifting my face, my arms
to the pregnant sky
spreading wide my fingers
until she births the rain
empties her fluid body onto
the skin of my mistakes
washing away pain and regret
replacing it with innocent
child-like laughter
I, spinning free of this sorrow,
releasing it to the air like
a pillow of weightless feathers
detaching from the shame
as if some kind of sacrament
was taking place
my scars falling away to be
forever buried and forgotten

and still, I dream of rainstorms
which offer such redemption.

JOYFUL SILENCE

Have you ever paused to listen
to the abstract silence, to hear
how the sky splits open at dawn,
how the cricket quiets as darkness fades
and dew rises from each blade of grass;

Have you heard the
unfolding of delicate petals,
wing's rhythmic vibrations,
the sprout of seed after
              an overnight trumpet of rain;

Have you heard the voices in trees,
a kernel escape from the sparrow's beak,
robins swallowing earthworms,
the pings of a wind chime?

Have you ever thought, as I, to be an
eternal slave to such silence
and yet be full of joy?

RELEASING SAD MEMORIES

I empty my mind of
yesterday's curse
try forcing out the
heavy stones,

I've carried these memories
like sad love songs
needing to be dissected
and rearranged, put back
together in such a way
that they resemble at least
some measure of love

I collect every catastrophe
every frayed fabric of misery
and hurl them all far from my reach
where they cannot cling to
tomorrow's hefty weight of
happiness about to immerge

CONSTRUCTION OF A POEM

I prop my lawn chair underneath
an elm near the brim of Pawnee Lake
my purpose to construct poems
out of trees
    and waves
        and cirrus clouds
out of outstretched sky
    the expanse of daylight
        a pair of nesting nuthatch
out of songbirds, paper thin
wings of bees and butterflies

out of fishing boats and pontoons
    jet skis skimming the surface
        echoes of children's laughter

from the glint of sunlight
scattered across these waters,
shining like priceless jewels,

long metallic bodies of
dragonflies zigzagging above
    the wet reflection,
from all external forces
    of nature colliding,
mingling in afternoon's breeze,
overlapping like the petals of
    unopened buds

Within that lovely portrait
a whimsical poem came forth
and made my face shine.

RIDING SUNSET

I ride the coattail of sunlit sky
tailgate closely in hopes of
finding where eternity begins

stopping for gasoline and
a bathroom break,
chatting briefly with the obese man
behind the counter who rings
up my purchase of Beer Nuts™
and energy drinks,
whose spirit is melancholy,
glassy-eyed wonderings etched
on his unshaven face,
his pudgy fingers punching
numbers on the register keys

maybe he too, like all of us,
is searching for more,
wishing to mosey on down
this stretch of highway,
follow the moving stream of
light into yonder, gaze upon her
dazzling display of color—
amber, violet, scarlet red,
the horizon gradually smothering her,
sky changing to indigo,
shadows sinking into this blue darkness

we seem forever engaged in the chase
for something our souls gravitate towards,
longing to secure a place we've not yet
discovered…so, we follow until the road
has given all it has to offer, until our souls
are granted freedom.

CAMPsite REVELATIONS

Daylight has relented
behind a silhouette of trees
and inconspicuous hills

Only a tinge of peach sky
remains before the darkness
chokes her down like
I chug this cheap wine

Little fires flicker across
the lake at occupied camp
sites, the smell drifts slowly
into my nylon shelter

The air is humble and generous
and enters my lungs like
a sentimental friend whose
only duty is to console my
troubled spirit

I've come here seeking
solitude, to ponder on
the mysteries of life, on
my own mortality and
what it all means

Instead of question it,
I can't help but to just be
present in this space, the
microscopic blip that I am,
so small compared to
the universe, so temporary

I want to record the sounds
so that I might replay them
while lying on my death bed,
when life requires nothing
more of me

The buzz of insects,
Water lapping at the shore,
hymns of birdsong,
howls of distant wolves,
splash of bluegill,
the sighs of nature

A final chime before
the termination,
when life is exhausted.

MORNING PARADISE

A pinhole of light fractures the morning
sun eventually slicing through this haze
like a shiny blade.
A cordial breeze fans away yesterday's worries,
making room for quiet reflection.
Clouds drag themselves wearily across the sky
occasionally interrupting daylight's sheen.
Swallows flitter with enthusiasm over green
and gold terrain, over the mirror of water
where I've taken solace.
The beach is quiet at eight a.m., no movement
just small references of creatures that have
tiptoed through last evening's darkness.
This tranquil scene embodies all that I seek,
all that makes my soul content,
a distinct resemblance to paradise.

RISING SUN

Sharp blade of daylight splices
open morning's sky
sun, that golden sphere, burns off
her early dew
luminescent canopy evokes
the buds into bloom
opaque petals of ruby red,
magenta, coral, and saffron
pink, amber, and lavender
as if a prism glints this countryside
a universe brimming with color
an overflowing palette spilling
pigment onto an otherwise dull
gray existence.

VIBRATING LIGHT

Ripple of sunlight
expanding across the pond
like a vibration

RIVER ROCKS

I kneel beside a narrow stream
under a shady elm
consider the assortment of
pebbles and stones lying just
beneath the surface as if a
compilation of yesterday's memories

Some jagged, mysteriously displaced,
gray and sharp, able to cut
like a serrated knife,
the sudden sting left as
a reminder, a gaping wound

Others dappled and smooth,
the edges filed down and softened
by the steadily flowing current,
round and polished as if given
special attention to the details

Still others stand out like shiny
crystals when rays of light bleed
through weighty branches
of emerald leaves, like shimmering
precious gems scattered about

These stones a representation of
landmarks left in the wake of living,
fulfillments and bereavements,
embedded joys and sorrows,
a generous handful of river rocks.

This collection of poems and prose is born of everyday observations and of a wandering mind. The vastness of nature has always been one of my biggest sources of inspiration; the elements that make up this planet in which we reside, but often neglect to examine and enjoy.

Words cannot do justice in describing the complexities of such a magnificent and profound world, although I have made a feeble attempt to do so with this book. I hope you have taken much delight in reading them.

Look for more books of poetry by Merci Lane Press in the near future! Until then, go out and explore this bountiful creation, paying special attention to the intricate details.

www.ingramcontent.com/pod-product-compliance
Lightning Source LLC
Chambersburg PA
CBHW030154070426
42447CB00032B/1188